A IS FOR THE AMERICAS

by Cynthia Chin-Lee and Terri de la Peña

illustrations by Enrique O. Sánchez

ORCHARD BOOKS   NEW YORK

To Sandra Hays and Devin Chin-Lee, who got
me started with the idea—C.C.

In memory of Sister María Guadalupe, who
suggested that I write a children's book
someday —T.D.L.P.

To Joan—E.O.S.

The flags on these two pages belong to the following countries:
FIRST ROW, from left to right: St. Kitts and Nevis, Colombia, Dominica,
Guatemala, Argentina
SECOND ROW: Brazil, Nicaragua, Cuba, Paraguay, Barbados
THIRD ROW: Jamaica, United States, El Salvador, Guyana, Peru
FOURTH ROW: Mexico, Ecuador, St. Lucia, Uruguay, Bahamas
FIFTH ROW: Dominican Republic, Canada, Costa Rica, Trinidad and
Tobago, Chile
SIXTH ROW: Venezuela, Antigua and Barbuda, Belize, Grenada,
St. Vincent and the Grenadines
LAST ROW: Suriname, Bolivia, Haiti, Panama, Honduras

NOTE: Some lands in the Americas are dependencies of other
countries, hence their flags are not included here. They are Anguilla,
Aruba and the Netherlands Antilles, British Virgin Islands, Cayman
Islands, French Guiana, Guadeloupe, Martinique, Montserrat, Puerto
Rico, St. Eustatius, St. Martin, the Turks and Caicos Islands, and the
U.S. Virgin Islands.

Orchard Books, A Grolier Company
95 Madison Avenue, New York, NY 10016

Manufactured in the United States of America
Printed and bound by Phoenix Color Corp. Book design by
Mina Greenstein. The text of this book is set in 15 point Baker Signet.
The illustrations are acrylic and gouache paintings.
10 9 8 7 6 5 4 3 2 1

Library of Congress Cataloging-in-Publication Data
Chin-Lee, Cynthia. A is for the Americas / by Cynthia Chin-Lee and Terri
de la Peña ; illustrated by Enrique O. Sánchez. p. cm.
Summary: An alphabetical introduction to the history, geography, and
culture of the Americas.
ISBN 0-531-30194-X (trade : alk. paper).—
ISBN 0-531-33194-6 (lib. bdg. : alk. paper)
1. America—Miscellanea—Juvenile literature. 2. English language—
Alphabet—Juvenile literature. 3. Spanish language—Alphabet—Juvenile
literature. [1. America. 2. Alphabet.] I. Peña, Terri de la, date.
II. Sánchez, Enrique O., date, ill. III. Title.
E18.7.C48 1999 970—dc21 99-11720

A Note on the Americas and Their Languages

Even though citizens of the United States are typically called "Americans," the term "American" applies to all peoples of the New World. This region includes thirty-five countries and thirteen dependencies in North, Central, and South America, as well as the Caribbean. These countries include Mexico, Canada, Peru, Argentina, and Brazil; the dependencies, for example, include Puerto Rico (U.S.), the Virgin Islands (U.S.), the Virgin Islands (Britain), Aruba (Netherlands), and Martinique (France). The entire area south of the U.S.—from Mexico to Cape Horn, including the islands of the Caribbean Sea—is considered Latin America.

The most popular language in the Americas is Spanish, spoken in most of Central and South America, Mexico, parts of the Caribbean, and in many areas of the United States. English is the most common language in the United States, Canada, and Jamaica, while French is spoken in Haiti, Guadeloupe, Martinique, French Guiana, and parts of Canada. Portuguese is the official language of Brazil, and Dutch is the official language of Suriname.

At the time of Columbus, there were thought to be more than two thousand indigenous languages. Native American languages are divided into eleven large groupings: American Arctic-Paleosiberian, Andean Equatorial, Aztec Tanoan, Gê-Pano-Carib, Hokan, Macro-Algonquian, Macro-Chibchan, Macro-Otomanguean, Macro-Siouan, Na-Dene, and Penutian.

A is for the Americas, North, Central, and South. Called the New World, the Americas are younger than Asia, Europe, or Africa. The first people to live here came from Asia by foot or by boat. These first Americans are called Native Americans or American Indians. Thousands of years later, people from other lands arrived.

The Americas have the world's longest chain of mountains, the Andes, stretching from Panama and Venezuela to Cape Horn, and the world's largest river and rain forest, the Amazon. Called the "lungs of the earth," the amazing Amazon is responsible for about one-third of the earth's oxygen and is home to fifteen hundred species of birds.

B is for bison, sometimes called buffalo. For hundreds of years, native peoples such as Lakota Sioux followed these big, shaggy animals across the Great Plains of North America. They ate bison meat and used the woolly hides for blankets. In Canada's Wood Buffalo National Park, the largest remaining herd of bison roam.

C is for Carnival, a festival of wild merrymaking. Costumed dancers parade through the streets in Rio de Janeiro and other major cities of South America as well as in New Orleans, Louisiana, where the celebration is known as Mardi Gras. Carnival marks the last day before Lent, the forty-day period before the Christian Easter.

D is for El Día de los Muertos, Day of the Dead, a holiday widely celebrated throughout the Spanish-speaking world. Mexican families decorate cemeteries with paper streamers and bright marigold bouquets. To remember and celebrate the people they loved, the families pray at the graves and picnic on the favorite foods of those who died. In some regions, children wear skeleton masks and buy skull-shaped pastries and candies.

E is for empanada, a turnover filled with spicy meat, vegetables, or fruit. They are a Central American specialty, although empanadas can also be found in Chile, Argentina, and Cuba. They come bite-sized (*empanadillas*) or as large as a pie (*empanada gallega*), and can be served as a complete meal, as a snack, or for dessert.

F is for *fútbol,* a sport popular throughout the world, but especially in Latin America, where many championship teams play. Known as soccer in the United States, *fútbol* is played by two teams of eleven players each. Each team tries to get the ball into the opposing team's goal, using any part of the body except the hands and arms.

G is for gaucho, the cowboy of Las Pampas, the Argentinean plains. To catch a cow, the gaucho swings a bola, a long leather cord with three stone balls on the ends. Whizzing through the air, the bola tangles around the cow's legs and stops the animal without hurting it.

H is for *horchata*, a refreshing drink made of nuts or grains and sweetened with sugar and cinnamon. *Horchata* comes in several flavors such as *horchata de arroz* (rice) and *horchata de almendras* (almonds). *Horchata* originated in Spain, but is now enjoyed throughout the Americas and is most popular in Central America, Mexico, and the Caribbean.

I is for igloo, a home for the Inuit, or Eskimo, people of North America. During the summer, igloos might be tents covered with skins; in the wintertime, they might be houses made of stone, wood, sod, or ice. Common in northern Canada, the domed igloos made of ice are built with entrances below ground so that warm indoor air cannot escape. The walls are insulated with furs. Light comes through openings in the top.

J is for jalapeño, a green chile pepper with a very hot flavor. Named after Jalapa, the capital of Vera Cruz, Mexico, it is popular in the foods of Mexico and the southwestern United States.

K is for kayak, a small watertight canoe. The first kayaks, developed by the Inuit, were made from a light wooden frame. They were covered by skins, except for a small opening in the center, and were used for hunting and fishing. Adapted for modern water sports, the kayak is part of many events in the summer Olympics.

L is for Lake Titicaca, the highest navigable lake in the world. On the border between Peru and Bolivia, this lake glistens at a height of twelve thousand feet (3,800 meters) above sea level. One of the islands in the lake, Isla del Sol, has beautiful coves and white sandy beaches. Inca legend says the mighty sun itself was born here on the island of the sun.

M is for maize, the Taino name for corn. For thousands of years, maize has been the basic food for native peoples of the Americas. Farming tribes, from modern-day Arizona to Nicaragua, grow maize to feed themselves and to trade the surplus crops for other necessities. Tortillas are made by shelling and grinding the maize on a metate, a special stone used for this purpose. Native people celebrate the growing and harvesting of corn with religious ceremonies and dances.

N is for Niagara Falls, a thundering mountain of water. On the border between Ontario, Canada, and New York State, Niagara Falls is about two hundred feet high (61 meters) and pumps out 20 million gallons (75.6 million liters) of water per minute. Daredevils of the past rode the falls inside wooden barrels, often with disastrous results. To enjoy the misty splendor, millions of visitors each year take boat rides beneath the falls.

O is for ocelot, night hunter of the forest. Covered with dark, chainlike bands of fur, the ocelot excels at climbing and running. Ocelots are found from Texas to Argentina. They feed on birds, reptiles, and small mammals.

P is for posada, an inn or dwelling place. Traditionally, in Mexico and in many other countries of the Americas, families and friends enact Las Posadas during the nine nights before la Navidad, Christmas. One group pretends to be the innkeeper and his family. The others, representing Mary and Joseph, the parents of Baby Jesus, pretend to be travelers. Outside, they sing and ask for lodging. The singing continues from house to house each night until the final night, when the people inside open the door and finally welcome them in. Everyone shares a meal and gathers to break the piñata, a decorated clay or papier-mâché pot filled with candies and gifts. Las Posadas is still celebrated today, but the festivities usually take place in a church or school and last for only one night.

Q is for quetzal, a tropical bird prized for its striking blue and green feathers. Found in the highlands of Guatemala, the quetzal is known for its brilliant colors and long tail feathers. The Toltec people worshipped Quetzalcoatl, god of wind and learning, represented by a snake covered with quetzal feathers.

R is for Rio Grande, the "big river," or Rio Bravo as it is called in Mexico. Separating the southwestern United States from the northern states of Mexico, the big river flows from the San Juan Mountains in southwest Colorado, through Big Bend National Park in Texas, to the Gulf of Mexico. Although the Rio Grande divides the U.S. and Mexico, it also is a shared resource, providing precious water for both.

S is for salsa, the sassy, jazzy music of Cuba that combines Spanish and African rhythms. Dancers sway to the rhythm of the conga, swing to the trill of the trumpet, cha-cha to the beat of the drums. On a crowded dance floor, couples dip and whirl, twisting in an endless series of spins and turns. Salsa rhythms can also be heard in the music of other Spanish-speaking countries.

T is for totem, the tree trunk that tells a story. The Tlingit artists of Alaska and British Columbia carve and paint totems, animal and human forms, on cedar poles. The Tlingits do not worship the totems they make. Instead, they tell their clan's history and legends through them. Some of the faces found on totems are ravens, eagles, owls, and bears—the animals they use to represent their clans.

U is for uakari, a rare, endangered monkey of the Amazon rain forest. Uakaris are small, short-tailed monkeys with bare faces. They blush when they get excited. Living in small groups in the higher branches of the rain forest canopy, they are sometimes kept as pets by the native peoples of the Amazon.

V is for Vodou (VOH-doo), a way of life. In Haiti, Vodou is not only a religion with African and Roman Catholic roots, but also a culture. Colonial landowners viewed the widespread practice of vodou among their slaves as a challenge to their authority and set out to destroy it. This persecution played a major role in the slave revolt that led to the formation of the republic of Haiti in 1804. Through singing, dancing, and drumming, the Haitian people today continue to cry out for freedom, faith, and tolerance in new and old Vodou traditions.

W is for wampum, beads made from polished shells. Pierced and strung, wampum beads were used for money, jewelry, and as a way of recording treaties by native peoples in North America.

X is for Xangô, god of thunder. Xangô is one of the gods of *candomblé,* a mixture of African religions practiced in Brazil. In the festivals of *candomblé,* its followers dress up as the goddesses and gods—the royal family—of their African roots.

Y is for Yucatan, a peninsula jutting into the Gulf of Mexico. The Yucatan is known for the huge pyramids built by the ancient Mayan peoples. The most famous stands in Chichén Itzá (pronounced chee-chin eetza). At their observatory in the Yucatan, the Mayans studied the planets and stars, creating an accurate calendar that predicted eclipses of the sun and the moon.

Z is for Zuñi, a native people of New Mexico. Living in adobe villages called pueblos, many Zuñi are master artisans. They make silver and turquoise jewelry and carve animal fetishes of tiny stone bears, ravens, and desert tortoises. In religious ceremonies, Zuñi men wear colorful masks and costumes to impersonate kachinas, the spirits of nature.

The Spanish-language alphabet also includes three additional characters that the English-language alphabet does not. These are Ch, Ll, and Ñ.*

Ch is for *churros,* a sweet, crispy snack. Street vendors in Latin America sell this delicious treat from their carts at markets and fairs. They mix a dough of flour, salt, and water, then squirt the dough from a pastry bag into a vat of hot oil. In a few seconds, they pull out a crisp brown stick, which they sprinkle with powdered sugar.

Ll is for llama, an American cousin of the camel. Native to the Andes, the South American mountain range, llamas are used as pack animals, and their shaggy coats are spun into wool for blankets and jackets.

Ñ is for *ñandú,* the largest bird in the Americas. The *ñandú,* or rhea, looks like a small ostrich. About five feet tall (1.5 meters), the *ñandú* lives in Brazil, Uruguay, Paraguay, and Argentina. The male *ñandú* makes a good father. He creates a nest by scraping a hole in the ground and lining it with grass. After the hens lay their eggs, the male *ñandú* hatches the eggs and cares for the babies.

* Ch and Ll will lose their designation as separate letters of the Spanish-language alphabet in the year 2000.